PRAISE FOR
DOING DRIVE-BYS
ON HOW TO LOVE IN THE MIDWEST

"The best writers are those who inspire me to write like they do. Whitman affected me this way, and Dickinson did, and so did T.S. Eliot. Reading Curtis L. Crisler's *Doing Drive-bys on How to Love in the Midwest*, I want to make his wild one-of-a-kind poetic voice my own, and I want to write about what he writes about, the world that needs to be written about, the world ignored by too many people, the world of brutality against the good people deprived of justice and love."

—John Guzlowski, author of *Echoes of Tattered Tongues*

"If you've ever wondered what it means to be a poet writing in the Midwest, wonder and wander no longer. *Doing Drive-bys on How to Love in the Midwest* is about loving, losing, and honoring the moments of life we do have. Curtis L. Crisler writes with an "urban Midwestern sensibility," that takes us in and out of April snow, an IHOP, the white and black of Indiana. Even more than that, this poet, in poems that move with breath and jazz across the page, asks us to consider what it means to be human, to really be human, when Black lives are being lost at an alarming rate, Breonna Taylor, George Floyd, Emmitt Till, when a global pandemic swallows us whole, when death comes too soon. In "Fifty Something Years of ~~Letters~~ Laters," the poet imagines a world where Emmett Till had lived and says: 'If she would not have lied / it's also possible I would not be thankful.' Here we should stand up and clap for the wisdom of this aging speaker—his perspective on this life, now, in this place, holds us accountable to find all the 'beautiful things' that will break our hearts."

—Sarah Sandman, author of *The Sinew of 47 Years* and *I Speak Moan*

"Listen: If you manage to put down Curtis L. Crisler's *Doing Drive-bys on How to Love in the Midwest* for even a minute—and I don't believe you can—you had best bury that sucker under a collected Shakespeare or a ten-pound anvil. Otherwise, this man's poems are liable to jump right up off the page and dance, so infused are they with righteous rhythms. But the moves aren't just for show. Crisler is after the heart and the hurt inside the contemporary experience. And so, he puts capital-R "Reality" on direct notice: there is some serious shit going on here we need to discuss."
—Justin Hamm, author of *Drinking Guinness With the Dead*

"All the feels I've ever felt about what it means to live and love and lay claim to the Midwest are expressed in Curtis L. Crisler's poetry. This is what it is to be seen. From the laments for George and Breonna and all the others we have never known, to the contemplation of corporeal and material ruin, to the excavation of passions dug down deep—all is laid bare here. *Doing Drive-bys on How to Love in the Midwest* is not just another addition to a stunning oeuvre. It is a message, a critical intervention, a rapturous ode to a way of being."
—Terrion L. Williamson, Director, Black Midwest Initiative, & Associate Professor, Black Studies and Gender and Women's Studies

DOING DRIVE-BYS ON HOW TO LOVE IN THE MIDWEST

CURTIS L. CRISLER

POETRY

C&R Press
Conscious & Responsible

All Rights Reserved

Printed in the United States of America

First Edition
2 3 4 5 6 7 8 9

Selections of up to two pages may be reproduced without permission. To reproduce more than two pages of any one portion of this book write to C&R Press publishers John Gosslee and Andrew Sullivan.

Copyright ©2023 CURTIS L. CRISLER

ISBN 978-1-949540-49-9
LCCN 2022952044

C&R Press
Conscious & Responsible
crpress.org

For special discounted bulk purchases, please contact sales@crpress.org

DOING DRIVE-BYS ON HOW TO LOVE IN THE MIDWEST

TABLE OF CONTENTS

/////
Sometimes it Snows in April — 11
where do all the fucks go? — 13
When a Sista Claims Her Own Damn Wand — 14
"A Bullet Hole in the Soap Dish" — 15
Looking for Hurston in a Triptych — 22
Fifty Something Years of ~~Letters~~ Laters — 27

/////
LETTERS TO REALITY (responding for the provinces) — 37
Dear Reality #2: — 38
Dear R #141: — 39
Dear Reality #0: — 40
Dear R #299: — 41
Dear Reality #67: — 42
Dear R #70: — 43
Dear R #273: — 44

/////
Venus Risen — 48
The Alchemy of Jailbirds — 50
When 2 Close 2 Tiger's Stripes — 52
Killer Bs — 54
Doing Drive-bys on How to Love in the Midwest — 55
Old Dude — 61
When Our Dead Asks Us to Come Visit — 62
The Automatism of *Reflection on Creation and Space* — 63
Tao of Aging — 67
Skin Rash — 68
How We Get Out — 70

/////
Crushed by the Love of Friends	76
What I am Looking for Amongst Midwestern Ruins	79
A Comforter / A Monday / & Little Bodies	83
Your Voice Has Too Many Bumble Bees	84
Stupid humans	86
there are times when i must let depression walk	87
A Navy Déjà vu	88

/////
in this uncertain space/ segmental light, compartmental time	92

/Notes/	96
/Acknowledgements/	98
/Biographical Information/	100

Dedicated to Aubrey McCaskell Jr. & Jon Tribble. For all you were & are to us.

/////

Hey me. From birth, we've postulated, from a bird's eye view, there's nothing on earth worth taking a life for, outside of self-preservation, maybe. Yet, many will grind in us their various justifications for taking people out. These moments are like napalm in our throat. Still, you fight against this truth. Nothing is sacred when facts are ribboned packages of snake oil. Day and night are/is. Yet, you justify, through faulty intellect, to be right over all else, even with your gods that you placate in creaky pews on Sunday. The lie is you. The lie is me. The lie is us grieving for some gold dust from our mother's mouth, as if prayer. It's just that prayers and hopes, these days, seem disbanded through the barrels of freshly smoking guns.

Sometimes it Snows in April

The snow f e l l like a miffed god took bites of cumulus clouds—spat them down from heaven, o n t o my Midwest — an idyllic snow-globe realm. The s n o w-covered the branches, pulpy, thick like a l l the trees were Douglas Firs. It was April 20th. There were blossoms bursting o u t of branches, headed towards spring, blanketing a chronic white on white commotion. Love t o o k me straight to Prince. A day before 5th anniversary of the guitar player relocating to another plane. I b u m p e d his b a c kbeat like meth. Every *body* antsy. *My city under resuscitation.* "Here Comes the Rain Again"—the next song in my ears. Annie Lennox knew proper way to p l a c e metaphors on v i o l i n strings. I r o d e around— this would be the last snow until the next snow. There's nothing like love in a car, being in the s n o w, letting m u s i c have me and bring me back. The officer who k i l l e d George Floyd will s e e bars. That's history. *There's that.* There's how Minnesota, people around the g l o b e, exposed their voices like a universal tsunami — people morphed into army of harmony. The snow moved me into Sun Ra. He, and band, birthed hallucinations of "Images." The ache of imagery, too much—so my tears talked. Broken,

recouping, I drove deeper. I videoed life like a young lady did outside storefront, but it wasn't enough to hone the scratchy emotions unable to escape,

acquiesce to good trouble. The emails. The texts. The chatter. M i s s me with that. I drove deeper. The snow talked in syllabic rumbles. Sun Ra

played for our mystic futures, out there. I pointed car towards Minnesota. Drove for *out there*. And I never pumped the brakes.

where do all the fucks go?

they fall   out our pockets with   loose dirt and old lent / they disappear with   the ice in our sweaty glass of dr. pepper / they fall out   the maple trees—the helicopters   the twisters the whirligigs   actually called samaras / they are hidden with   the voices in tulsa's   mass graves / they go where they go when we   vacuum the dust bunnies / fucks float like hopes, we must care and believe in them or   else they shy and hide   like tinker bell, feeling some   type of way / they move with the shadows because they too are shadows / they used to bend down to a child's level   until the child started looking   like his daddy / they fall fast and hard like lies we say aren't lies,   but grow heavier now—blame   yo mama / they get lost in phrases like i will never hit you again / they jingle with the loose change as we   make left turns in our minivan, while our children yell yeeeaaaaa / they evaporate in moondust tarrying into the night / they   hansel and gretel our childhood   for a place deep   into the woods of our psyche / they   go missing with i thought i had 20 bucks in my wallet / they linger   in shrubbery with our stalker / they fall into our mouth—loud residencies full of elephants,   full of donkeys / they live in the cloudy   eyes of a person cold-cocked while still standing, while the brain has broken rank / they fall in between the identities of the theys who   were hes and shes last year / they say one thing to   our husband and another thing to   our priest, but we don't find out until we are on our   deathbed / they have changed their taste, but will say they   taste the same / they're squirrels and possums and racoons working   2nd shift at the factory / they are lodged in the breaths   of smokers of joggers of swimmers checking for   their heartbeats / they trickle down and ferment   in the taint, just so   we will scratch / they slide out a   mother's slippage when identifying her son's body—evaporate into our blue sky /

CURTIS L. CRISLER

When a Sista Claims Her Own Damn Wand
—for Susan Howard

I bet there's something Hogwarts about where
you'll be smiling now. Maybe Dumbledore is your

ferryboat guide, waiting with your mother and
father and Jesus. A goblet for you. A chilled bottle

of sauvignon blanc in his other hand. *Something
to cleanse your palate for your journey.* And it is

Dumbledore, not Sir Michael Gambon, all robed-out
by the funky-lit bus station from out of bad film noire.

Getting old is knowing old is coming—growing

skin tags and moles riding the roadmap of your
epidermis. These specks appear like spring blooms—

whenever. These specks ride you on out until your
eyes turn off, not some predicted age you believed

you would die at. So hard the monotonous
mathematics of death—that twirling of our time—

that twirling of white wine, releasing flavor's blast.
That woeful trumpet, brilliant at sending you off.

"A Bullet Hole in the Soap Dish"

You view today, "working
out," with a slight wind from

    the northwest, raising soft
    hairs on the back of your neck

        or blessing your forehead.
        There's no immediate sweat-

            beads soaking your handkerchief
            like wet grinds in a filter.

                People merging back to "new
                normal" like voiceful traffic

                    on I-69 at 5pm. Yes, it is
                    Friday. What I'm getting at is…

you believe today "copacetic" —
a good day, like Ice Cube.

Until, an elderly white woman
with a round, white, stomach, lays

lifeless, on filthy Walmart floor,
off Coldwater Road. She gets

CPR by EMS, whose inter-
twined hands try jumpstarting

her battery. How stark the contrast
between his rhythm of pushing

down—two skin colors co-op-
erating in this time of BLM.

What I'm getting at is…
pandemics are frustrating

when you're trying to reboot
life, restart breathing. When it

    slows to crawl—the only
    motion in real-time is

        a round, white, belly and
        big, black, hands pushing

            an elderly white woman
            down into the earth. It all

                appears anime-ish when you

                    walk away, into the sunshine

                        of a 77-degree day, where
                        a firetruck looks too large,

                            red as ever, with real, lemon,
                            sunbeam-lights obstructing

view. Two more paramedics
assist an elderly white man

at the driver's door of his SUV.
What I'm getting at is...

it looks like the beginning of
a mad zombie or sad infection

horror movie, where a few
people fall dead before the out-

break spreads. It's end-times.
You can taste apocalypse

with a pandemic between
two slices of this existence.

It feels, almost, almost
there—fingertips

stretching to grasp
this out-of-reach

encounter. On tv,
Giannis Antetokounmpo

and the Bucks lose 115-100,
to Jimmy Butler and

the Heat. Afterwards,
on your tv, *The New*

York Times Presents:
"The Killing of

Breonna Taylor"
(S:1, E:3). Everything

slurries into narrative—a lie,
the bullets, the March

13th killing—around the
time corona puffs out its

    jowls full of venom. Life
    slows when her mother

        remembers going into Breonna's
        apartment, detailing where

            the bullets ran through things.
            What I'm getting at is....

momentum impacts you, an
18-wheeler—steel meets body,

    in solar plexus. All the sun
    of your day doesn't mean

        your day revealed any light.
        You can't purge the white belly

from brain. You can't purge being
asleep, at home, while Five-O

with 'no knock warrant' will wreck,
knock down door to domicile,

wake you from sleep, to put
you down forever. All tomorrows,

Breonna's never-bes. All days
after, Breonna's should've beens.

Looking for Hurston in a Triptych

I. Zora (letter one)

You were your name before you were
named. I went old school, dropping things
in the mail. That is why I'm coming to you—
to know your failures as much as your goldens.
You have become the *it* & the *they* & the *we*.
Hell, I'm feeling all kinds of broken—the hour
that includes the minutes & its seconds—
the forest that includes its animals & its trees.
The computer, its motherboards & its chips.
The screams of us—our terrors & our heart-
aches. But, still, there is no name for how we
lose. Hell, we lost you before we found you.

I am burnt raw—in machinations where you smile under the brim of your hat.

I wanted God to rearrange the matrix.
Thought he'd do that Superman thing—
go backwards, around the world, &
put words back into their proper lexicon,
make time cooperate? But God ain't down
with human commands. You would have
conquered the world, & we'd have it all:
the Eiffel Tower, consciousness & blue
note, the Euphrates, a harvest from seedlings
to how black life gave its birth dazzle—
the language of babies still learning to jazz.

There were no women with your tongue & your color kicking anthropology & ethnography.

I'm writing to you because I'm a boy with

a flat line, in a man's body. I'm searching for
that *Mule Bone* glow—before it all went
south—for a phrase from another black
woman because it's always black women
who save me. If you were dead, I wouldn't ask.
How are you with this new migration, *this*
blackness? Today, again, I play in your name—
in the tepid water puddles, letting the sun
dry me naturally because this poem's all natural.
More sunflower than bougainvillea blooms
about the earth surrounding me. More dandelion
than juniper. It seems you know something
about dying, about living, about resurrection.

So, I'm calling out to you: Harlem Renaissance, Niggerati, Janie, Tea Cake, Barracoon.

II. Before You (letter two)

I am looking at you while
I'm looking for you. I may not
have stated it correctly in my last
missive. It's hard writing to someone

who's too busy to reply. I'll keep doing so
                until you say stop. I know you are

getting them. I know you are reading
them. I know it bothers you too—
all this world. You know, it's like you
created Florida, with all that Eatonville

patois—a sound that reverberates through
the womb, like coming out of a tunneled
slide, a child with bubbles in her stomach—
that echo of release. That's where I'm at,

succumbing to your trickster smile & what's
                behind your eyes. I see there's a convoluted

aura mixed with the mud and thickets of
resilience—then, some. Now, what am I
to understand about a black woman discarded
like the unwanted touch a child's never to

talk about? I mean, they couldn't find you,
your gravesite, the life you owned—until
they did. You weren't even on the record.
You were lost. Then, you were found. Now,

there's a headstone. Now, there's your books
                taking up space in Barnes & Nobles,

in university classes with a swelter of minds
determining you should be constellations, or
some closer connection to our solar system.
I am improvising, in the cut, figuring out

the how, the to, the why of where water enters
& where it breathes before it leaves or
evaporates. All I'm doing is evaporating like
a song fades, then there's nothing but the needle

in the groove keeping time. Somedays all
       the beautiful things in my life break my heart.

III. All Up In This (the Zora dreams)

You come to me like the night trying
to hide the moon—halfway out its pocket.
I can see night's hand caressing its rim.
But, maybe the way I'm seeing it doesn't
sound like a perfect sphere. My sights a little
off, correcting from the blare of all day
laptop screens, & I don't have my readers
on. Motion can fool you into believing
you're in a minefield full of poppies,
& you are high & low, simultaneously,
dragging your nightmares into daylight.

You come to me like the day moon—
try to say it isn't bloated on passion—
so heated, it rises like a Chinese
lantern left to float into airspace to show
everyone a soul can rise. This is my soul,
lifting into the blue, stretching my arms
across the sky to hug you forever.
I never knew how to demonstrate love
when it's just us. So, today, I'm trying to
hide the sun in my pocket. It's hot,
for sure. I love yellow—to grab passion,
place it next to my 49¢ & have the coins
burn their imprints into my thigh. Only
this abuse can satisfy the ache from the sun,
the smoke from my bones. In the heap
left stirring, you won't recognize me.
You won't find any lies lifted from my ashes,
before the wind propels me about
the air, singeing with your name.

Fifty Something Years of ~~Letters~~ Laters
—my paradoxical absolution of Emmett Till

I have two dreams of us. The first, we are sitting
at Navy Pier—lost in the old barges and ships,

when white smog from the mills isn't fogging up
our view. Still, we're in a whiteout of seagulls, diving

for our turkeyburgers and sweet potato fries.
You're telling me about the grandbabies. Miss

Mamie didn't let them run the streets of Chi-town
without her. Everybody they grew up knowing

knew Nana Till's voice too. We met cause a buddy of
mine married a friend of yours. I call breeziness.

The flapping wings of seagulls. The air full of lake
spray and sulfur. This letter starts farther down

the right margin. I don't know, maybe getting older
puts weight on one's shoulders. Funny to say.

You carry us like a mother carries her newborn,
from hospital into this undulating madness, scared

like her frame's full of flames. There are so many of you
and you're only one of you. I am returning to you

like the hawk returns from surveillance, soaring—
not a disturbed flapping of its windblown wings.

It soars, lets the wind uplift it just by breezing.
I am brought back to you, Emmett, cause Carolyn

Bryant said "Nothing that boy did could ever justify
what happened to him." She only said it fifty-

three-years too late. Some documenter, Tim, got
her to reveal lie she placed in secret locket under

    her sternum. With flying birds, the sternum, or
breastplate, is attached to muscles that give to

        flight. Carolyn was grounded. She placed lie inside
trinket her heart smothered in. She said nothing

            for light years. Your mouth full of snakes, twigs,
and mud. Not a whistle in you. She lived with her

                lie like it was the family dog—day in, day out,
until there were no more days for barking.

                    She outlived giving up her special to a killer she
knew was the killer. I can never escape dreaming about

                        you Em. I wanted to write to you. I'd try being
missive, but I don't know man. I'm shit at

                            elocution. What's real too, I am shit at avoiding your
probing eyes under that smooth fedora, soliciting

feedback on all that's been going down, up north. They killing a lot of boys that look like you Em. They killing brown women too. They look like your Mama, Miss Mamie. Sorry for being lax in my initiative. I'm that new kind of lazy—lost—jaded. It's probably due to not seeing Miss Mamie when she came to the church I used to attend in Fort Wayne. I was too tired. But what's more tired than death? I had all these questions lined up. What kind of sparrow or wren flew near her windows that reminded her of you? Or did she ever move that new outfit she put out for your return? How long did it sit on your bed without you in it? I had all these hugs I gathered from my shelf and put in a bookbag.

Then, came the headaches—the second set of dreams.
You smacked against my brain, dislodged pebbles of

rubble-sense I thought I owned. You did so much—
a martyr who didn't know he would matter.

I couldn't tell Miss Mamie about the second set of
dreams. How everyone in them had your face, full

of Tallahatchie River, a bullet, left-over bruises—
the gin fan's barbed wire groove dug deep into

your neck. Their motivation to hold you down in
the silt and grime snapped, got lodged on happenstance.

In these dreams—the deconstruction of your
boyhood—the side-by-side pics of you in killer

fedora, next to you decimated in a coffin—so
panoramic, this black and white. *Jet Magazine*—

a subscription to another world. Dreams of your
river face. It was your face on my mother, when she

turned around and said hi. It was your face on
my sisters—coming at me, trying to catch me

as I tried to run away. It was your face on my best friends
faces, throwing your river head to each other. It was your

face on my woman, wailing in gurgles, legs clamping
me down into all her special. It's weird to be so old

and new—me talking to a fourteen-year-old, when
you're older than me. What's that? What can I

do before my bones become the only information
all up in me. You are all up in me, like love, is

what I am struggling to say. I hope you're laughing
at that. So hard, you shoot milk out your nose.

I see you in your mother like I see me in my mother.
I wish they could've met. Man, Carolyn actually

said, "Nothing that boy did could ever justify what
happened to him." I know. I know. But it seems we just

collecting bodies. A smoking red river full of bodies.
Yeah, she was scared. But damn. I don't know Em.

This sax loving my ears. *This bass strumming tendrils*
I didn't know I had. *This drum*, my heartbeat.

It always takes 30, 40, 50 years, if ever, to get
a justice-slice. *Em? If she would not have lied,*

it's also possible I would not be thankful.

/ / / / / /

It's the little things, *globs of people say. That's what you'll miss, me. The smell of rain-drenched hair in your nose, staining your shirt and pillow with petrichor and Gloria Vanderbilt, or her stale morning breath you inhale when kissing before leaving. So, you're not lonely. You've had it all but are without it, for the moment. You will whimper at this anatomy of reminiscence, like a dog set free miles away from home. Yet, the next night, the bedraggled animal will show back up on its stoop, full, with sad eyes—groveling. This is us. Not just us but everyone. We can never escape ourselves. Be it danger or safety, we burn our own effigies. We even strike the match to light the flame that subsides the chill in us for some heat. We are wonderful miscreants. We run away from us, daily, but at the end of the day, we return, back there—home.*

LETTERS TO REALITY (responding for the provinces)

Dear Reality #2:

I had written the last word before I had written the first word. I have died with Sichuan's province, as children bury their parents, and parents bury their children, looking for answers in a gray rubble. You have taken my soul back to Tangshan. I have the impossible rise in 3-D, have heard the Dolby (surround sound) of lives echo in the aftermath. I cannot think of Tibet, of the Olympics. *Can China and America be related?* I am caught in web of blackness, permanently shut eyes. I am not impressed with pyrotechnics, creative body counts. This is not a blockbuster cinematic-event; families become orphans, the landscape lopsided, due to your traverse to make it a slew-footed cow, a poor lifeless chicken, or ubiquitous fallen egret.

I have heard many rumors and can do nothing in America because we are shuddering simultaneously. How can I marry the pain of the man alive for three days under rubble of buildings, reaching out a hand, telling his voice to go on without him, but his body does not concede? It moves along the sound waves of his voice, like a musical note, on a scale, for an apt musician who plays familiar melody in Indiana. I cannot take you all up in my face. Even at this distance, you are still too near me, and my television booms its HD, so I cower to a world where Nature whirrs and hums, dancing her cha-cha on wet tectonic plates.

Dear R #141:

You never wrote me back after the last letter, or if you did, it made no sense to wait for your lack of an acidic rebuttal, so I'm sending this one with a SASE. *Are you so self-involved you can't "man-up," take a moment to go give a name to the faces that have been booking my dreams since the whirling?* Dammit! *Must I go over your head for consensus? Or, are you so damn sure that the faces of the people I dream of only belong to time?* What about Africa, India—other lands where you leave your seed of regret in feral earth, leave the babies of bastard terrain? I know, I know. I should be less direct and more forgiving, that would be the Christian thing, but I am no Red-Cross. Yes, I know. I should walk like a ballerina here.

The darkness in me wants light, the dove rising from black cave to the little eye that shines like a perfect moon on the first night I asked you to fire up the wick; yet instead, you blow hot between the lines. It's how you say nothing so loudly that screams.

Dear Reality #0:

Our rivers have mutinied here. They have risen-up and clapped their hands and poured all they know onto the earth, and houses are rich in water, silt, and soil. Midwesterners take boats down the boulevard to get mail, and lose themselves in the day-to-day, mirroring the day-to-day of the morning prayers from those sparrow mouths in China. Nature, she is mad, and I believe her husband has done an impropriety that the world is paying for. Or maybe, she is just sad in her menopause, how we don't communicate with her, *the trees, the skies, and the waters are beautiful as always.*

This falls on us. Now, we grieve at her backlash for our frog's song.

Dear R #299:

There is always so much to say. I lost my voice in the silence of our last ticking second. I know you are the narcissist, beyond the max. *Why get your wig on just to be crooked?* Your shaking disrupts getting all mailings, changing of diapers, and brushing of teeth. *Can you ever focus on the obscure from your point of view?* Maybe that is rhetorical. Out of focus has clarity with those left behind. And *live?* fervent like breath. The landscape in the province proves this. I can see yellow lights from Indiana.

I never want to see you again R. I mean this dissent, on all seven levels.

Dear Reality #67:

All of this has happened before in my dreams, when I was the crow, but you make dreams feel so new—materialized. I never knew you were so close to home, symbiotic with all air, all seas, and all dirt particles. I knew you as a raised eyebrow, never to be discussed in public squares. Legend told me you used to be a friend to these moments—the now—today.

I once lived as a bare somnambulist, foraging for blurry faces to straighten up a hyper-clarity.

Are you always present in the same tense? Or, are you just a baby in the moment before becoming an adult? I am fascinated, but will not correspond with you again, for I have lost my mind at your insistence for pleas like a bastard child to a long-ago father.

Dear R #70:

I know I said I would never write again, but the faces in my head will not stay buried. I wish you'd answer my calls, but a robot keeps sending me to voicemail—disconnected—strange happy grudge. Bodies have risen in Midwestern water to a mountainous large in Sichuan—so so high, and I couldn't advance further in this war for justification. I am meandering if you will give reference for the next uprooting. I would like to prepare for questions I have no answers too. I'm sure if I heard your voice I could reconcile how to justify this madness since you are a harbinger about your outcomes.

If you get this in time, take a moment to reintroduce yourself to perspective. I'm sure there are taste buds you haven't used. Maybe, if you aren't hiding out, you can blame me for lacking the knowledge for tomorrow.

Dear R #273:

I cannot believe your aftershock. How could you send this to me, to the faces in my dreams? If you are so dishonorable in your affection for me, I will not concede. I will go above your head to strain your neck at my wingspan. I have blessings on a decorative mountainous shelf, waiting for an inoculation of this nature. I have tried with you. I have lied for you. But I have died too many times, lost in a window looking out, into the front yard of your heart, with nothing but smudgy, dirty, filth lain on the floor of an Indiana dining-room—the kitchen of Sichuan newlyweds.

You do not love us. I get that. I really do get that. But faces have a currency with me. I will let you go, so I can go back to meaning. Dreaming those faces will mend China and America, and stitch up a hole, a burden handed out to a little boy on the Yangtze, to the small girl on shores of the Mississippi.

/ / / / /

It's hard to even listen to the poet's spit, now. Their grieving of bruised fruit, cold in their crispers, recognized but put off till later. You learn how we discard the self. If you're not eating fruit, you're not eating fruit. It's much easier to switch it out for new than to cut out what's dying.

Everything comes much slower, me. What's lonely and lovely overlaps—the unfitted sheet folded back over the top of the quilt—a fifty-dollar bill, in a wallet, President Grant kissing his own face.

Venus Risen

i.

*What's more beautiful
than knowing your own destruction
is left up to you?*

*Nothing
loves anymore,
if it ever loved since breath's first mourning.*

*We are all demi-gods rallying
to become legit gods—
monsters.*

*It's funny, my mother's house is
going through its own menopause.*

*I'd accept her hands, their psalms,
even if she's never abandoned revenge.*

*Still, I miss
Mami's smile
saying morning.*

*All this time,
I never dared this
living would be so inflexible.*

Still, it flutters. It waves.

ii.

I believe I am
a cicada. I lived four times
through seventeen-year

cycles of
want I must
devour to continue surviving, even

as death is my light. In this silence,
I languish. When the radios
are off,

the podcasts quiet, and I'm not
pissed at lack of synergy with our social

construct of civility—cicadas
sizzle—flexing our tymbal organs

and wings, an orchestral
fluidity of release—seventeen

years worth. I have
done this four times
now. What's crumbled

me, pokes up in
heartache like pointy, sharp,
antagonism. Still, I dream,

my superpower is getting
believers to really see.

The Alchemy of Jailbirds

On our love-making-bed, our sleeping-bed,
you lay lovely, naked, as moonshine

thieves through in slivers, like pick-up-stick
limbs from winter trees. It is cold outside.

There is a meanness to our social application—
the way we cut off people's necks with a look.

It is January—and COVID. The streetlights
sticking out along and around the curve of

the road jutting up like raised hairs on chill-
bumps, glinting into our window. I sit and I look

and I listen as your breasts rise, fall. This
living. I know air scatters all of the micro-dust

and particles all around us. It reminds me
of the only time a parent can sigh, feel secure—

when the baby is asleep, chest rising and
falling, and you watch down on her—dumb

and numb. You wonder…*is this what God does
all day?* Try understanding all those little

difficulties with living. Try understanding
the loud deceit of what makes us move, go on,

and push all that hurt out. It is January. It is
cold in this world, at this time. At this moment,

when you turn over, your breath hesitates,
is interrupted due to readjusting. You pull the

covers over most of your body, legs still
naked, needing. Somehow, you trust *me* to watch

over your breathing—all over again. I wait
until you regulate and snore out a cacophony

of baby noise. I'm stuck in our finality too.
It is cold in the world, and January hollers.

When 2 Close 2 Tiger's Stripes

If anything, we should be trying to
kick the n i c o t i n e, with patches,

doing d u e diligence under neath
our skin that m a r k s us like a

bully's beat - down w o u n d s. If
anything,   we   should be trying to

stop drinking darkliquor swimming
with Coke or Pepsi, with breakfast.

Our eggs   never taste like starting-
the-day-right anymore. If anything,

we should stop making metham-
phetamines our main   absolution

when with our daughter at the
k i d d i e park on a four-hour visit.

There's f a c t o r s,   then there's
FACTORS.FACTORSgowithusing,

do not g i v e ½ a d a m n for us,
or the ceaseless,smart, p a i n. It's a

Bengal tiger, rotating its shoulders,
creeping into our bedroom in the

middle of the night as we look for
focus, realize her g u t t u r a l purr

tingles our   testicles—the real fear.
We care to shut out what   our two

eyes adjust to, but we   get mesme-
rized by her muscles, her objective.

Her eyes, a wonderment of yellow
reaching for us as we ossify and

piss and shitourselves.Her dripping
s a l i v a catches all   moonlight, a

paradigm of celestial   God-watch-
ing—diamonds e m i t t i n g their

brilliance. Her g i r t h 's atop   us.
We smell r a n k breath. We f e e l

her vibration and it feels like the
bed won't h o l d up. We   don't

move. We   can't move. She places
us i n t o her mouth — n o t h i n g

sexual about   death. It is power and
s t e a l t h and the magnificence of

hunting bringing us   together. This
is dominance.This is a l l about her,

animal on animal, teeth inour meat.

Killer Bs

There are 99 ballerinas searching
for the home they are running away
from—vigilantes in this apocalypse because
no one could hear their angry feet,
cracked, with broken and reset toes—
crooked and disformed for the rest
of their serviceable existence. They continue
to spin no matter what. Often, they crumble
in kitchens and bedrooms. Always to
the groaning of men. All 'Rinas receive are
standing ovations by watchers robotic
to the tutu—faces like an LOL-smiling-emoji—
not a bit of sense running through what
doesn't grimace. *People ain't all one thing.*
The things you do to be a 'Rina when everyone
looks for some art to toe pointing in
pointe shoes. The art of chaînés. 'Rinas
are the silent army in the streets, taking out
double-takers with their powerful legs.
Their slippers embedded with razor-
blades. Their turns, ravage like razor wire.
Cinematic. Non-choreographed. They fast toe,
step-point, like a pat of flamingoes.
Heated. Full of that red blood
splashing about their faces and tights.
*We're all broken and taped like
yesterday was a waste.* The 'Rina's smile,
and sweat, 'cause they know it was not.

Doing Drive-bys on How to Love in the Midwest

vvvvvvvvvvvvvvv

We sat in Starbucks / filling our bladders before running to the restrooms because we were liquid-logged / A gaggle of white girls sat by us on a Friday / raised their feathered eye-brows / I was the only guy in that new establishment / They saw this brown man / me / with this white woman / you / I could hear their minds calculating so many scenarios about brown hands & what they do & don't do / so many reasons to call the sheriff / I had to rinse expectability / I looked at them & smiled / while I did my own computations / It was the day you kissed me / leaving a sliver of the sweet light of saliva on my cheek from your new medication's side effects / They don't know that / They don't know I'd kill for you / They don't know you wouldn't want me to kill for you / They don't know I'm your little bro & you're my big sis / No DNA alike / no same father / same mother / They don't know our type of family tree got different leaves / They don't know / we made a family out of a community of sharing our shards / I could start throwing dregs around Starbucks / giving into microaggression & its surrogate malevolence

/ I could get pissy / wait for cellphone after cellphone to report me to / the men outside ready to bum rush the "Black dude" / I can't have them take me away from you / They don't know Starbucks homes your no#1 coffee / I was just there because I drove you to your hot-spot / It was the day I saw Miles Davis' trumpet up for auction at Christies / on my Motorola / while you relieved yourself / *They're still looking at me* / I was looking at them / I was looking past the re-evaluated planting of philodendrons since the Cosby verdict / To them / my skin became a verdict / But I could not fall into leaves of depression from lying eyes / So I focused on Miles / Learning about his design of three personalized trumpets / all with his name on them / one for auction / one he left for the family / & one he had buried with him / I wondered what kind of song he'd play for me while my body moved slowly & all the girls & women stared at me in bully-tones / But I wasn't feeling like lunchmeat / not with you hosting me / I heard Miles rusting in his dingy casket / looked sideways for Coltrane or Rollins or Charlie to pitch up the melody / looked for Ella to do something elastic for this moment of aching / I wondered if I had his trumpet would I play it / *Would I place my lips where his lips had been?*

/ Would I know what a note was? / Would I know what the man was? / Would I know who I was? / What jazz is? / What I need in October? / On the 18th? / At 3:37p.m? / The women & girls cut their eyes / giggled out warning signals / Out the window all the men sat / capturing the warmth of the sun / We got up / & it seemed like I was a god / my body stardust / a neon-spectacular / from boy / to dust particles / You / a truckdriver / Bejeweled & new / like Bathsheba / We left them / smiling / We walked past the men / the light shining off their cars / into our carriage

/ We fell back into conversation about patriarchs & family trees / & the next thing I knew I was driving with north star / back home / after I dropped you off with a swarm of nuns / & nothing as sweet as the bitter cut of crisp October pulp / smelling like love / like I was born to belong /

Old Dude

There's desire, still,
sitting on the desk in my head,
next to the books I haven't gotten to—
titles & authors that lose out to
grandbabies & fewer friends.
I move like I move when I move—
turtling across time zones with more flesh.
I function like an old cigarette lighter,
even as I'm good at cleaning & oiling,
it still takes two to five times before
the flame becomes constant. It used to
only take once—then, a strong fire,
standing up like an orange, resolute, soldier
on watch. I look at my watch, & the
wonderfuls that I'll produce today
are the small things my daughters take
for granted. Bending is a magnificent
honor, now that I must warm up
to do it, else the pain in my back moans
something that will echo through
the caverns in my mouth. I remember
my grandfather made these noises
when he was my age—alive.
The water at the pond ripples today.
I wait for my daughters, who will
come by if they can break free from
their apropos activities. So, I wait. I wait
because the grandbabies make me
smile. They are so small, & bendy.
They come at me, like I'm candy,
like their joy will eat me up.

When Our Dead Asks Us to Come Visit
—for Jon & Aubrey

We still like driving on the highway, even though
        we must stop more to pee. Hydrate, & pee again

at gas stations adorned with Taco Bells or KFCs
        connected to them. & they're always in places that

end in "ville." We trek thirteen hours to honor our
        dead. Nothing cool to say about it. Just watching

each other between the crazy of conversation—
        catching up. Each time out of the car, November

whispers her brittle leaves against the concrete of
        everything—that breeze along our faces as well.

There are the ravaged cornfields, the emaciated
        soybeans, & the withered treelines riding with us,

like they're murals on windows—noticed stowaways,
        stopping when we stop. We smell nature, her arid

perfume of dirt & pollen. & we need to taste her.
        Not like the grime you taste in your mouth from a

bully shoving their dirty hands onto your lips. More
        on purpose. To bend to the earth. To take a knee.

Putting our pointing digit in our mouth for our saliva.
        Then, putting finger within the dirt, only to return

it back to wet mouth. We smack on elemental ingre-
        dients, & say, "That's earth. Real earth, my friend."

The Automatism of *Reflection on Creation and Space*
—a Triptych (featuring Alice Coltrane's symphonic aura)

a) …to my pillow…

Yes, there are the triggers. The flashing nights
I don't want to arbitrate, so I put new pillow-

case over the old pillowcase you are wearing.
It is not so simple, how your anger hovers

above my head like a dented, crooked, halo.
I put on Alice Coltrane. Her brown hands

talk to instruments. Her instruments talk to
us. We antagonistic—still. I've put minerals

and lotions and creams on my face, in my
hair, and they leave their oils and splotchy

excrements behind. This makes you frown.
It's like those days I wore a curl—looking

like Prince and MJ had a baby. Understand,
there were other pillows before you, when

I was wilding-out and didn't care to cover
up my junk, but *that* life had nothing to do

with *this* life. I come home for you. I lay my
head on your creases. I open up my palms

to caress the cool side of your underbelly—
to warm a naval. I dream on planes, in cars,

on ships about when I can wrap my legs
around you. So, know this. I never want to

quiet your fluff, your stubbornness. *I got you.*
I want to confide. I want to spend the rest

of my time fighting for, and with, just you.
There's no other place to ever lay me down.

b) ...to my bed...

The first time I spot your thickness—
your curves all out on the showroom floor.

You model it up. I tractor-beam to you,
bobble-heading stupid verbs men use to get

laid. I get interrupted by your handler.
He palms your body like a pervert. He talks

you up like he knows the celestial. He does
not own light perception. When he bounces,

I jump to you. I am full of piss. Full of moan.
Full of visualization of our future. Full of

showing-my-ass so I can observe yours.
We are so green, then. I appeal you don't get

irked by my taking out the black photo
album, fingering back through all our trials

and testimonies. Alice employs love fingers
on 88s, on the harp, wielding feminine through

a cornucopia of hardship. Your body's heavy,
firm. I am reluctant, vulnerable, off key,

but I'm getting naked first. I'm removing
Nana-Mama's quilt. I'm getting all up in them

sheets, pounded from our mercurial nature,
pulsing within Alice's rage for blue serenity.

c) ...to my quilt...

This is the second time I put you back on
the bed. It's me. I can't get enough you.

I am smoothing out the wrinkles on your
stomach, as you lay down on the body of

the bed. You all crisp, smiling in harp light,
moving in your patchwork of generational

wealth. I'm unashamed that this is midday,
Wednesday, and we have been doing this

for the last five years. I know I can't make
you mine. I'm not trying to. I want you how

I can have you. You are your own body.

I am good with all you let me participate in,
with you. As I tuck your corners, I see that

Alice did a two-record set—her music blows
out the speakers and blows on to you and

speaks to both of us in floral hieroglyphics.
Before I can leave, I put my face all in your

tragedies, triumphs, and secrets—a dad's
army dress jacket, a grandmother's white

wedding dress, and a baby's birth gown.
I'm impulsive about you too. I hear you sigh.

It sounds like a fingernail skating on silk.
I hear the wrrrhth! I hear your *please return*.

Tao of Aging

Them gray hairs unruly—
unjust, how they romp and
roam in a goatee, on a hair-
line, or in pubic arena. Glinting
a fine light. So fine, you can
see they are really refracting
today. Them gray hairs jack up
conformity. They can't stand
being a body next to a body
if they can't let their bodies work.
They jut to the left when strands
go right. They jut to the right
when strands go left. You brush
them together and they cackle,
first posing, aligning like they
a regiment—inspired. Then, they
jump and jag their jagged bodies
to protrude out from the symmetrical
line. You thought they were
teased to perfection. Oh no. They
morph their bodies like they broken
and bent, like tattered things,
like a shrubbery or a kindling ready
to set roof on fire. Gray hairs
don't give a shit about shit.
They are good with themselves—
individuals for life. They love
the parties. More show up like
some flash mob, like at Coachella,
letting pubes frolic about. You
can try dying them out, but them
roots will resurface like the
living dead—they pop up like
bad split ends or mean crab
grass—wiry—inconsolable.

Skin Rash

My body medical scar
My body mental scar
My body ancestor
My body (re)percussion
My body keloid
My body varicose
My body got mouth on it
My body see my body   my body
My body shatterproof
My body soft tissue
My body peacock
My body platypus
My body not yo body
My body target
My body focal point
My body want she's body
My body erect
My body intimidate
My body deterred
My body reprobate
My body clickbait
My body my body   I said
My body escape
My body cinematic
My body war
My body fire
My body squall
My body sparrow
My body retro
My body not yo body
My body calabash
My body bitterroot
My body chicory

My body questions
My body questions   questions
My body storyteller
My body stretch
My body protest
My body confess
My body undertow
My body thrash
My body hot take
My body burning bush

How We Get Out

Back in the day / back when they still lit matches to carcinogens up in IHOP / we sat there / Me / lost in cumulus cigarette smoke / & you / puffing out pale clouds like a Clydesdale running in the clarity of a winter's night / There is a smile to your aura / back then / That night you weep it lovely because the Fort Wayne Philharmonic orchestrated *your* music / Everyone at Progressive Baptist Church & the Fort Wayne community / got all the oboes / all the flutes & the clarinets / the tubas & the strings / all the liberty in your head / got a time stamp /

got a conductor / & you / collaborated with music's ostentatiousness / Back then / we had one IHOP / That night / instead of oral afterglow after the concert / we slid into the Hop & I looked at you looking at your sheet music like it was a naked woman / I asked / "So, how does it feel to hear mad voices in your head / like you've always heard them / & we, the misinformed, couldn't?" / "Man, that was Christ-like" / is what you said / The realest Christian-talk / People looked strangely to us / two dudes / geeked-out on stained sheet music / Me / hogging buttery pancakes & sausage / You /

runny eggs & toast / sugary
coffee / full up on hot smiles
deep down in freed
tendrils of your gut /

/////

From a worm's eye-view, you'll find the sex lopsided at times. Her lips, a flat C. Our temperatures hot like death-stars. Cataclysmic shifting of our loves and losses like bits of gravel in our shoes. Yet, we get comfortable with agitation, have our wobble down, love the voices riding our maladies of pseudo-individuality. No sponsors. No family. No lovers. No gods. Not with all this readjusting, all the influencers who don't influence love—just gnat-like voices. Smaller Us's, roiling—our heads, the ping pong balls in championship play.

Crushed by the Love of Friends

There's lucid grace about the sound of pee
against porcelain that makes me miss the friends

an epidemic won't let me visit. I close eyes
as my penis releases toxins and other irregularities

with forceful rhythms—even at this, the splash
invigorates through the release and call back.

One hand on my junk, the other on the coolness
of the wall. Here, I use this counterbalance to

stabilize any wobbling, else my thoughts get wet.
Friends always come down like angels at offbeat

angles in the restroom. The ammonia from the
urinal furnishes slight hints of wheat my sensitive

nose comprehends. I am no different from the
wrinkled-face man, a urinal over from me, breathing

with a crackling cough from somewhere within
the hinterlands of his chest. *Possibly some respiratory*

ailment, I contend. Eyes closed, my Spidey senses
hear the wrinkled-face man like the sonar of a dolphin

bouncing off a shark. He is something real at this
moment. At eyelevel, the tiles transform into plasma

screens my friends appear on. We ride along a hot
stretch of interstate to get to one another, to gather

hugs, compare hells. We let loose our janky ghost
like kindergartners released for recess. When we meet,

again, I love, consume friends, in bowls or plates of
food we will cook until we fall asleep on couches,

beds—up late afternoon the next day for a circuit
breakfast. We go out, let sun do us. Listen to Luther

at lunch. Listen to the rain splat after dinner, before
we don't say *good* or *bye* on Sunday. Then, I drive

and cry and sing for friends until our next focal point
appears. I don't mind the dark—sitting, laying in it,

as if I didn't pay my light bills. It is here I find
recompense—sniffing for answers I never knew were

truffles to me. I am the empath, or close to emphatic.
I will hurt your ears with R&B collections of torch-

songs torn through social distancing, to redistribute
how to touch graciousness with my flash-bang-love.

Did you see the NBA boycott? What I thought when I
heard about a friend's ascension. I wonder *do bodies*

trade like money exchanges? All these lines, tight hugs.
No need for a fixer. I am a delicate boneyard-of-hope.

Everybody dies on a day they never expected. Sirius
FM is a timeline in my blood—the hyacinths and lilies

of labor falling inside the snow-globe of a far-scape
enlarging my eyes. It's all the tea sips. All the Velcro.

All the releasing. All the inhaling, up my nose, now.
It's all shaking dicks 'til there's no urine left in my

urethra. There always is, especially when older. I am
lost in this gray forest of tile that is no TV screen.

Death comes daily. Like relieving boredom. Like
being next to Mr. Wrinkles. He leaves first, after

repacking himself. I grunt. I sigh. I readjust it all.
I am fortunate your faces don't fade from my mind.

What I am Looking for Amongst Midwestern Ruins
(the hallucinations of corona)

a/
I am **true north**, looking south.
The moss on the thirty-**nine trees**

in front of my apartment **faces** me,
tells me how to equivocate—today.

The bulbs thicken more and more
on the maples, the ashes—the leaning

birch, the fallen few logs woodpeckers,
sparrows, and robins posture on for

rest. **Today, April** the first. A piece
of birch moss lays on my patio. One

of the frenetic squirrels does circles
around the tree, probably **digging** its

claws in so deep that it's **kicking** back
bark onto where I live. Maybe not.

Nonetheless, it is there, on a concrete
patio, **showing** me how **Spring** will

have her say, corona or no corona.

b/
I am surrounded by
today. I am **surrounded**

by the artwork of my
mother, who painted a **jazz**
flowing wine, sluicing through

a flute glass—the red with
the orange against the white,

adding crystal to the glass—
haunts me. Three brothers named
Bailey, have placed their hands

on the covers and pages of
poetry books. Now they hang on

my walls to illustrate they will not
die. Why, I want to be a Bailey
too. The textural garmented

flight of fancy of Kipp Bailey's
three black women's gowns

rise off the cloth canvas—a blue
so naughty you want to touch.
More blue loves my living-room.

Blue Boulevard by Robert **Girrard**
hangs above my fireplace and

the lone man in forefront seems
to be walking out of the snow
into living-room, next to my picture

of **Satchmo** in 1900's golfing garb,
sitting down on some floor—

given to me by a friend with one leg,
now. Henri **Rousseau**'s *Sleeping
Gypsy* hangs above my bed.

Like the lion, there's **a connection**
because I'm the Leo in my

family. But I am also the man
sleeping next **to musical**
awareness. Aware and unaware,

simultaneously, like a usual,
hustled, parent. I am saved by these

artists, daily, falling to **sleep**
on my couch, uncumbered, or not,
just next to them. I am with

them and they are with me,
unconditionally, like a bag of hugs.

c/
Cloistered in
green moss—

a benevolent **loneliness,**

a salient gathering
of all of who we are

against the trees. Up on

tree's backs—**an all of
everything** I want and

do not want—
symbiotic pods

on long-limbed arms—

a fine liberation **wanting
its bloom.**

A Comforter / A Monday / & Little Bodies

The snow deputized Monday's moodiness / crunch by crunch / under boots / under an overcast firmament / My parka and gloves asked if I was warm / Uh-huh / The comforter / too much for my Maytag / got pelted with parachuting, slow-mo, white angels / falling to earth / like ash from chimneys / A Catholic lip balm if in stigmata / A papal remembrance / Nothing like religion to hold us hostage / Something mean about gas showers made me SMH / War, with its blotches / I hugged comforter, tighter, /before breaking threshold of laundromat / Transformed back to little / Carrying my smaller sister through projects / We, cold / Breath, Cloudy / I, big brother / made her laugh to forget winter / thrashing at her exposed nose and lips / to forget projects / I had no compulsion for shape-shifting / then / She was a sparkling little planet round my neck / A smile I hated to see cry / Something that frightened me / How parents lose their shit when the screen door shuts /and we / the children / are on fire, outside / No threats / other than Mother Nature / pushing us back / towards home / before other threats could pounce / But big bros crowd little sisters / I knew nothing of balance / That a multitude of feathers can hold some weight / Hell, I was fledgling too / "You watch the back. I got the front. Ok?" / "Ok," she boomeranged back, in little girl. "Nothing but a bunch of snow!" She laughed / I shook her body / She laughed harder/ In little bits / a comforter brought us back / Ghetto- kids shlepping through winds wanting to capture the heat from childhood / Now, my sis lives in Austin / Doesn't care to listen to January's sass / Is it because I'm not sludging / Mama's baby / in a bear-hug / through winter / to get us home? / No / her dreams grew hungrier / She just learned new ways to taste survival ///////

Your Voice Has Too Many Bumble Bees

We used to hear your libations. *What are*
the molecules coagulating within our blood

and cells? Are we safe, working over solder
pots with no safety-masks? Is it okay for

dentist to run behind a wall and push a button
while we sit there in radiation's sunshine?

If only we transform into Hulks. Not the case.
All the chemo, all the x-rays, has everyone

walking like limelight—exposed. Shadows of
ourselves have been talking to each other,

saying that we are losing our sense of connection
to the bodies we own. Fragmented, we turn

into rhinos, giraffes, and sloths. Animals
rummaging in Kroger for their grass fed this,

organic that, trying to keep up with doggies and cats—
some promise of life after our bodies have

been nuked like Hot Pockets. Animals move
beyond dim days of working in caves, in mills,

on railroads where their lungs are full of soot
and dark viciousness—a taproot in the bloodstream.

Animals will wonder, *Are we half? Half*
ourselves? Half our futures? What are the

molecules coagulating within our bone marrow?
The dentist tells us to return in six months. *Yes.*

*But what does NO mean? Funny how coalminers
and canaries hijack the consciousness.* We

look for prevention the more we are prescribed.
Drugs that dull the soundtracks of harpsichords—

the sterile, the metallic aftertaste—pills inform
all our smacking. We crave returning to spicy,

existence. Something salty, sweet. Something
golden. Something sticky. Something so less bland.

Stupid humans

We born
  We slobber
    We crawl
     We walk
Turn into stupid teenagers

      We stomach
        We spawn children
          See stupidity in rearview
            See responsibility on windshield
Our children have children

        We wrinkle
        We gray
        We die
          We eaten by carnivores
Our children, carnivorous

            Our children hunger
            Our children echo
              Our children greedy
                Our children crave
        Sweet meat of wildebeests

there are times when i must let depression walk

      when the lovers you love can't reciprocate
voltage. when your muscle memory rejects

      your brain's hand signals. or, when no one is
listening to the craggy woman on a megaphone

      screaming to a lazuline sky that *men are crazy
af—e'ry day*. somewhere, inside the wheres, is

      the meaning of "right here"—& there was a
conversation you made in the light. & the light &

      you made alterations on the future. when you
let go, wind massages your face like your favorite,

      old, addiction. & you do nothing to resist,
while the voices in your head shut up, & all

      the voices in real-life chat right up in front of
your back. no one sees you own all those voices—

      primal, young to fading—you own all the
thoughts, the dark liquor, the fixes to your elastic mind.

      there are times when you must listen to
listlessness, accept the loose whirr & rotation of the fan.

A Navy Déjà vu
—4 U

I have yet to meet this blues baby that is inciting all
Austin, Texas, the after-party-for-life. Actually, I have

met you, in the photosynthesis of my sister's brown eyes.
You are the oxygen produced in your father and mother's

love. I've never said, "hey you," to you because corona
stood up at the party, said, "hold up, wait a minute"—

like out of some 90's rap bridge. I see the pix, all cheeks,
looking back at my nephew, your mama—got you lifting

brows. *We trying to be cool, with Christmas happening*

*in the middle of this epidemic—with us having new love
on the map like love didn't know what mapping out love*

means—when most fearful. I'm really trying to govern
my lines with water, food, shelter—possibly a new onesie.

Honestly, these pix are holding us down. Honestly, you
can't even recognize the crazy we are. *We straight fools.*

Navy, dee jays playing the demo of your lungs—fresh
hope born in this apprehensive moment of tangled weeds.

Navy, 'til I smell milk-breath, I'm back kicking it with
treble clefs, in dirge, emoting inside my blue whole-notes.

/ / / / /

Life on this sphere is messy AF. In our Mind Palace, it's never how we dreamed or willed it. What's in your head, is a life. What's outside your head, another life—two different worlds. And get this, everyone in these worlds choking on the same, damn, machinations. We're all broken, it's nothing more human than that.

in this uncertain space/ segmental light, compartmental time

  in this

      uncertain space,

                between birth & death,

    we need

        hope as surely

            as we need

                    food & water;

                in her

          eyes, she

      suffers lifetimes;

                doctors can't explain

                        why some girls

                                    enter puberty sooner;

                  consult a pediatric

                        textbook

                            & you'll learn,

    nothing is

surreal
   until it actually happens;
                    "you mean
                        my mother
                            didn't destroy the world?";
                        the acrylic
                   paint on my
              walls of memory
is clear?;
      if instinct
          can be trusted,
                stupid people
              are often
      dangerously sure
of themselves;
    & if any one
           asks who you
                are, the standard
                          response will be _____ ;

/NOTES/

pages (9. 35, 46, 74, and 91): These sections are dialogues from the narrator to his younger self about the ins and outs of their existence on this place we call earth, up till now.

page (14): "When a Sista Claims Her Own Damn Wand" is a tribute to Susan Elaine Howard, R.I.P. (April 9, 1961-October 20, 2021).

page (15): The title of the poem, "A Bullet Hole in the Soap Dish," comes from Breonna Taylor's mother, Tamika Palmer, from the *New York Times Present: The Killing of Breonna Taylor (S:1, E:3)*. She reflects on what she saw once they let her into her daughter's home. #SayHer Name—Breonna Taylor! R.I.P. (June 5, 1993-March 13, 2020).

page (22): In "Looking for Hurston in a Triptych," I use, at the end of section two, the phrase "Somedays all/the beautiful things in my life break my heart." It comes from the line "On some days, all of the beautiful things in my life break my heart." This comes from the Season 2 (series finale) of *Lodge 49*. https://www.youtube.com/watch?v=6osM4wOQa8I.

pages (37-44): In "LETTERS TO REALITY (responding for the provinces)," the narrator uses the epistolary form to convey to Reality how perturbed he is due to the devastation of the 7.9 magnitude earthquake that hit on May 12, 2008, in Eastern Sichuan, China, (killing 69,195 people, injuring 374,177, and with 18,392 missing and presumed dead). The Eastern Sichuan earthquake is married with the 2008 June and July Midwest floods in Iowa, Illinois, Indiana, Michigan, Minnesota, Missouri, Ohio, and Wisconsin (killing 16 people, and causing $6 billion in property damage) (*NOAA; USGS*). Those three months still affects us on so many levels.

National Oceanic and Atmospheric Administration. "2008 Midwestern U.S. Floods." National Climatic Data Center. Web. 30 Dec. 2015.<http://www.ncdc.noaa.gov/extremeevents/special reports/2008-Midwestern-US-Floods.pdf>

USGS: Science for a Changing World. Earthquake Hazards Program. Web. 30 Dec 2015. <http://earthquake.usgs.gov/earthquakes/eqinthenews/2008/us2008ryan>.

page (48): "Venus Risen" is a tribute to the fabulous poet Venus Thrash. R.I.P. (March 30, 1969-June 19, 2021).

page (63): The poem "The Automatism of *Reflection on Creation and Space*" was taken from Alice Coltrane's 1973 album *Reflection on Creation and Space (A Five-Year View)*. R.I.P. (Aug. 27, 1937-Jan. 12, 2007). *Note:* Playing the album while reading the poem is recommended.

page (84): The title for the poem, "Your voice has too many bumble bees," comes from the anime *Welcome to the Wayne*.

page (91): "We're all broken, it's nothing more human than that" comes from *Altered Carbon, (S:2, E:8)* "Broken Angels."

page (93): The poem "in this uncertain space/ segmental light, compartmental time" is a cento comprised of phrases from arbitrary books.

/ACKNOWLEDGEMENTS/

The following poems have appeared in some form in the following journals, magazines, anthologies, etc. **BELT Magazine** for "Sometimes it Snows in April." **Cherry Castle Publishing** published a video on YouTube (https://www.youtub e.com/watch?v=0WFO-q4XcZM) of "A Navy Déjà vu," under the title, "Navy Déjà vu." **Cider Press Review** for "Tao of Aging." **Last Stanza Poetry Journal, Issue #1** for "Old Dude," "What I'm Looking for Amongst Midwestern Ruins (the hallucinations of corona)," and "When Our Dead Asks Us to Come Visit." **Last Stanza Poetry Journal, Issue #3** for "A Bullet Hole in the Soap Dish." **Our Common Suffering: Anthology of Poets in Memoriam 2008 Sichuan Earthquake.** "LETTERS TO REALITY (responding for the provinces)." **The Indianapolis Review** for "Killer Bs." **The Langston Hughes Review** for "Looking for Hurston in a Triptych." **RHINO** for "Fifty Something Years of ~~Letters~~ Laters," which also won a RHINO Founders' Prize.

This manuscript could not have come to fruition without the support of Purdue Fort Wayne (PFW), the PFW English & Linguistics Department, PFW faculty and students, PFW's *Confluence*, the PFW Faculty/Student Reading Series, the Indiana Chitlin Circuit, Professors & Pathways (P&P), Young Scholars Academy (YSA), The Multicultural Center, The Office of Diversity, Equity, and Inclusion (ODEI), Helmke Library (faculty/staff), the Fort Wayne and Northeast Indiana community, and the future movers and shakers I have worked with while developing this manuscript.

Love, honor, and respect to family, friends, activists, those still standing/dealing with COVID, those we've lost to COVID, others we've lost for different reasons—Aubrey McCaskell, Jon Tribble (and Al for sharing him with us), Tasha Bushnell, Jerry Lawson (and so so many more); to **C&R Press** for digging my work, Cinema Center, Allen County Public Library (ACPL); Allen County

Juvenile Center (ACJC); The Black Midwest Initiative (2nd Biennial Black Midwest Symposium), meeting Terrion L. Williamson F2F, Hanif Abdurraqib (O.G. Columbus), Aaron Foley (O.G. Detroit), Tamara Winfrey-Harris (O.G. G.I.), avery r. young, Aisha Ford, bree gant, DeMar Walker, catching up with Duriel E. Harris, (and to all the Black Midwesterners supporting and doing their thangs); Cave Canem for the *Cave Canem 25th Anniversary* and the online workshops; Ed Roberson for picking my poem, "Fifty Something Years of ~~Letters~~ Laters," for the RHINO Founders' Prize, (and RHINO, again); Wunderkammer CO.; Kanela: (Jazzetry: Spoken Word Open Mic: First Friday); Hyde Brothers Book Store (Last Thursday Reading Series); Dan Swartz, Omowale Ketu Oladuwa, Clydia Early, RasAmen Oladuwa, Michael F. Patterson, Chief Condra Ridley, Emmanuel Ortiz, Teresa Vazquez, TehilaYah Ysrayl, Scott Sprunger, Mary Quigley, Jack Jones, Marsi Lawson, Rhonda Meriwether, Paula Ashe, Laurie Gray, Cookye Rutledge, Michelle Chambers, Mari Hardacre, Leslie Anne Mcilroy, Tom Hunley, Kevin McKelvey, Liz Whiteacre, Adrian Matejka, Brett Griffiths, Kathryn Young (for making this possible), DuEwa Frazier (creator of Nerdacity Podcast), Mary E. Nance, Ryan Schnurr, Cheryl Scott-Fields, Dr. Sarah Sandman, Mary Elizabeth Encabo, Dr. Shannon Bischoff, Dr. MarTeze Hammonds, Shanté Howard, Carrie Adams, Crystal Purcell, and to the people I have not mentioned by name, you are not forgotten, you matter—you are part of this too. Know that! There's no way anyone of us does "good trouble" alone. Bless you ALL!

/Biographical Information/

Curtis L. Crisler was born and raised in Gary, Indiana. He received a BA in English, with a minor in Theatre, from Indiana University-Purdue University Fort Wayne (IPFW, now PFW), and he received his MFA from Southern Illinois University Carbondale. An award-winning poet/author, Crisler's *Doing Drive-Bys on How to Love in the Midwest* won the C&R Press Award for Poetry. His other books are (with Kevin McKelvey's) *Indiana Nocturnes: Our Rural and Urban Patchwork*; *THe GReY aLBuM [PoeMS]*, published by Steel Toe Books; *Don't Moan So Much (Stevie): A Poetry Musiquarium;*"*This*" *Ameri-can-ah; Pulling Scabs*, nominated for Pushcart. His YA books are *Tough Boy Sonatas* and *Dreamist*: a mixed-genre novel. His poetry chapbooks are *Black Achilles*; *Wonderkind*, nominated for a Pushcart; *Soundtrack to Latchkey Boy*; *Spill*, won a Keyhole Chapbook Award; and *Burnt Offering of a City*, won the Kathy Young Chapbook Award. Crisler's awarded fellowships and residencies are from the City of Asylum/ Pittsburgh (COA/P), a Cave Canem (Fellow), the Virginia Center for the Creative Arts (VCCA), Soul Mountain, a guest resident at Hamline University, a guest resident at Words on the Go, and Writer-in-Residence (Writers @ The Carr Program) sponsored by Poets & Writers, INC. Crisler's awarded grants and awards are a Library Scholars Grant Award, a RHINO Founder's Award, Indiana Arts Commission Grants, Eric Hoffer Awards, the Sterling Plumpp First Voices Poetry Award, and he was nominated for the Eliot Rosewater Award and a Jessie Redmon Fauset Book Award. He's been a Contributing Poetry Editor for Aquarius Press and a Poetry Editor for Human Equity through Art (HEArt). Crisler is Professor of English at Purdue University Fort Wayne. Contact him for readings, workshops, presentations, panels, etc., at poetcrisler.com.

CURTIS L. CRISLER

Printed in the USA
CPSIA information can be obtained
at www.ICGtesting.com
LVHW090419170824
788482LV00004B/414